Department of Health and Social S[...]

Diagnosis of Child Sexual Abuse:
Guidance for Doctors

Prepared by the Standing Medical Advisory Committee for
the Secretaries of State for Social Services and Wales

London   Her Majesty's Stationery Office

© Crown copyright 1988
First published 1988

ISBN 0 11 321155 4

Contents

Diagnosis of Child Sexual Abuse: Guidance for Doctors

Page	Section
1	1 Background
1	2 Introduction
2	3 Epidemiology
4	4 Responsibility of Health Authorities/Health Boards
5	5 General Principles
6	6 Talking to Parents
7	7 Presentation
7	8 Grounds for Suspicion
10	9 Initial Response and Strategy Discussion
11	10 Interviewing the Child
12	11 Confidentiality & Consent
15	12 Physical Examination
21	13 Role of the Psychiatrist
23	14 Role of the Family Doctor
25	15 Training
26	16 Research
26	17 Staffing Implications
28	18 Conclusions & Recommendations

Appendices

33	A	List of Members of Working Party
34	B	Advice on Confidentiality/Child Abuse from the Co-ordinating Committee of the UK Defence Organisations
37	C	The Initial Medical Contact's Role – Flow Chart
38	D	Relationship of Perpetrators to Children of All Ages: Pie Chart
39	E	The Medical Report
42	F	Training Materials
43	G	References

1 BACKGROUND

1.1 As a result of the Cleveland cases, which were the subject of great media interest in the summer of 1987, the Secretary of State decided to set up a judicial inquiry into the matter. He also asked his Standing Medical Advisory Committee (SMAC) to draw up guidance for the medical profession on diagnosis of child sexual abuse, and they decided to set up a working party. (Appendix A contains the list of members). The working party met on 10 occasions, studied the literature on the subject, and had discussions with other experts in the field.

1.2 Definition

The working party decided to adopt the definition of child sexual abuse used in 'Child Abuse: Working Together'[1] (DHSS) originated by Schechter and Roberge[2] and later adopted by Kempe and Kempe[3]:

> 'The involvement of dependent, developmentally immature children and adolescents in sexual activities they do not truly comprehend, to which they are unable to give informed consent; or which violate social taboos of family roles'.

This category of abuse is not exhaustive, nor is it mutually exclusive of other types of abuse, such as physical abuse. It encompasses all those activities in which children are used for the sexual gratification of older people. This includes attempts at or commission of vaginal, anal or oral intercourse and the introduction of objects or fingers in the anal or vaginal orifices. Fondling of childrens' genitalia or the involvement of children in pornography is also covered by the general definition.

2 INTRODUCTION

2.1 Widespread recognition of child sexual abuse (CSA) has occurred only recently. One of the first reports of its existence as a major hazard to child health was in France in 1886 by Paul Bernard[4]. In this country the present laws on incest were enacted from the 1890s onwards in response to growing public anxiety, but in all probability CSA has been present in our society for centuries. In a similar way, 40 years ago non-accidental injury in childhood (NAI) was not regarded as a major problem, even though many of its features had been published in a medical journal as early as 1860 by Professor Tardieu[5] in Paris, and the advice he gave then is still relevant today — eg if the doctors are called in they should tell the police, and pathologists should not be surprised at anything they see.

2.2 Following the work of Caffey, Kempe and others[6] in the early 1950s the syndrome of NAI became universally recognised as an important condition affecting children especially in the early years of life. As a result District Health Authorities (DHAs) now have rules of procedure and local advisory guidelines to deal with the problem.

2.3 The problem of child sexual abuse was rarely reported until the last decade when it began to be more generally recognised. Many cases occur within the family circle[7]. (See Appendix D). One of the major differences with child sexual abuse is that physical signs are not such a constant feature as in NAI, making a certain diagnosis more difficult.
The medical aspects are only one element in the diagnostic process.

2.4 It is now agreed that the problem has to be faced as a major one by all concerned with providing services for the health of children in the community. More than any other condition adversely affecting the health of children, **child sexual abuse requires close co-operation and exchange of information between the services, agencies and different types of professionals who are concerned with the overall well-being of children.**

2.5 The need to identify cases, make an accurate diagnosis and take appropriate action should be obvious. Child sexual abuse can have serious lasting effects: problems with sexual adjustment, interpersonal relationships, educational achievements, a wide range of behavioural symptoms and difficulties with self-concept[8]. The diagnosis must be made and action taken against the knowledge that a mistaken diagnosis can be destructive to future child and family happiness. Failure to recognise the problem can lead to continuing severe and unnecessary distress in the child.

3 EPIDEMIOLOGY

3.1 Whatever the shortcomings of existing statistics, it is clear that there has been a considerable increase in recent years in the number of reported cases. This is due to a variety of factors, not least to the climate of opinion which makes it easier for children to express their distress to concerned adults. There is a growing awareness of the subject, both in professionals and with the public. In 1985, the NSPCC dealt with 1,586 registered cases of child sexual abuse in the 11 areas where they manage the child abuse registers, which cover 9 per cent of the total child population of England and Wales. In 1986 and 1987 the comparable figures are 2,137 and 2,304.

3.2 Prevalence

In this context this is usually taken to be the proportion or percentage of the adult population who have suffered CSA at any time during childhood. Prevalence studies therefore rely on information from adults about events in their childhood. In this country there are no reliable prevalence data.

A useful paper analysing the available studies in the UK has recently been published in 'Health Trends'[9]. The paper demonstrates the pitfalls and unreliability of such studies: eg each uses widely differing definitions of child sexual abuse, and the respondents are not a random sample of the general population. The same problems were found in studies undertaken in the USA[10].

3.3 Incidence

The incidence rate is defined as the number of new cases occurring in a population during a single year. In this country, there are no national statistics of incidence.

3.4 Although there are no reliable figures for prevalence and incidence, certain points emerge from present studies.
a. As CSA is not always reported, available figures underestimate the situation.
b. Better awareness and willingness to confront the problem on the part of professionals is allowing more children and parents to disclose abuse. There is also improved recognition of such problems by those close to or working with children.
c. The problem, as with NAI in the last thirty years, requires the development of new ways of working with other professionals and

with other agencies, so that the best interests of children and their families may be served. These measures cannot wait for attempts to produce accurate figures for the prevalence and incidence of CSA.

4 RESPONSIBILITY OF HEALTH AUTHORITIES/HEALTH BOARDS

4.1 No one body, group, organisation or individual can be solely responsible for the identification of cases of CSA and the administrative and management procedures which follow such identification. We support the principles laid down in 'Child Abuse: Working Together'[1] (DHSS).

4.2 These explain that local authorities and their social services departments have primary responsibility for the care and protection of children including those who may have suffered abuse. The NSPCC and the police also have statutory duties and powers for the protection of children. All these agencies and health authorities have independent functions and professional objectives in the matter.

4.3 Each social services Area will have an Area Child Protection Committee (ACPC), formerly known as Area Review Committee, on which all the agencies involved are represented at a senior level. The District Health Authority should agree policy and procedures, to be contained in written documents, which should complement the policy on the management of child abuse agreed by the ACPC, and copies of these should be made available as necessary. **All doctors including family doctors should be familiar with the local ACPC policy and the DHA handbook.**

4.4 The community child health services, the paediatric units and the departments of child psychiatry should identify named individuals who are responsible for implementation of policy on CSA in their department. It will also be necessary to identify doctors with the necessary skills and experience to deal with the clinical aspects of this condition. Inevitably, in many districts this will mean the creation of training programmes, as such skills and experience are not currently widely available. It must be recognised by DHAs and individual professional staff members that accepting responsibility for these cases represents accepting an additional work-load and time commitment.

5 GENERAL PRINCIPLES (see also flow chart in Appendix C)

5.1 All doctors who work with children may come to know of or suspect CSA in one of their patients. It is no longer reasonable for a doctor to expect never to see a case. This is not only true in the family practitioner and hospital paediatric services, but also in the Community Health Services, Departments of Accident and Emergency, Sexually Transmitted Diseases, Gynaecology and Child and Family Psychiatry.

5.2 Just as in every other condition in medicine, accurate diagnosis depends on a careful history and relevant clinical examination. This must be followed by an assessment of what investigations might be needed and how to use referral for specialist opinion. Time should be spent planning strategy. **It is unusual for the diagnosis to be made on physical signs alone (see paragraph 12.19).** No doctor should feel isolated and unable to discuss worrying cases in an informal way with a colleague who has expertise in this field.

5.3 Hurried intervention may cause more harm to the child and the family. There is rarely a need for immediate detailed clinical examination. In the majority of cases this can be organised with deliberation so that the emotional trauma to the child is minimal, and the examination is conducted by a person who is skilled and experienced in this branch of paediatric (and forensic) medicine.
Repeated examinations at this initial stage should be avoided.

5.4 Doctors should be aware that the probability of finding definite clinical evidence is low, but absence of signs does not mean that CSA has not taken place. It cannot be over-emphasised that legal proof does not necessarily depend on medical evidence. Even in the absence of any clinical findings there may well be other and adequate evidence of CSA.

5.5 Medical assessment should be part of a multi-disciplinary process which includes a full family and social history.

5.6 Confidentiality is defined in the same terms for all doctors irrespective of their particular branch of the profession, and they should be prepared to justify their actions. However, medical confidentiality must not work against protection of the child (see section 11 and Appendix B). The child should be seen clearly as the patient.

5.7 The statutory responsibility for removal of a child from its family lies with social services. However, this action should follow recommendations by the professionals from the agencies involved in the case. It is rarely necessary to remove the child unless it is thought that the child is in physical danger or may become so.

5.8 The main responsibilities of a doctor involved in a suspected case include seeking further advice and information and keeping an accurate record of what is known, or has been found. In particular the doctor should contribute to case conferences, and attend court if requested.

5.9 Further training and updating will be needed for most doctors, especially in respect of normal child anatomy. Doctors who are likely to be involved in the full physical examination may need training in the collection and presentation of evidence.

6 TALKING TO PARENTS

Involving parents in discussion should follow the usual principles of good clinical practice. In a case of suspected child sexual abuse they should be given every opportunity to communicate their worries and concerns in a non-emotive atmosphere. A differential diagnosis should be fully discussed, and even in those cases where the parents are suspected of being the perpetrators of the abuse, the doctor should not adopt an accusatory stance. If further investigation is required, the reasons should be fully explained and the parents informed of the results. It is important to maintain positive relationships with the parents as far as possible throughout the whole process of the enquiry.

7 PRESENTATION

7.1 Emergencies

When the child first presents, the history may initially suggest that it is an emergency. On further investigation the situation may prove not to be so urgent. Thus the immediate removal of the child to a place of safety is in the majority of cases not necessary, and must always be weighed against the emotional damage which separation might do to the child and the family.

But immediate removal may have to be *considered* where the child
a. has suffered recent severe physical or emotional damage
b. has disclosed the identity of the perpetrator, and a return home may expose the child to significant risk of re-abuse, physical harm or pressures to change their story.

7.2 Non-emergencies

In many cases a child will present to a family doctor, school teacher, health visitor, social worker or at a hospital accident and emergency, paediatric or other specialist department, and be found to have a story or symptoms or signs which cause CSA to be suspected. It is rare for it to be necessary to set in motion the procedure for urgent removal of the child from the family setting (See flow chart in Appendix C).

8 GROUNDS FOR SUSPICION

8.1 Disclosure from child

Once an allegation or disclosure, of actual or suspected abuse is made to a doctor, the onus is on that doctor to take further action. It is important to take what the child says very seriously, and to spend time listening to what the child has to say. Some children may be in danger if they return home, (see 7.1(b)) and urgent discussion will be needed with professionals working in local child abuse services. Arrangements should be made for expert interview and examination. A video can be a helpful way of recording such interviews.

8.2 Information or allegations from others

These may be parents, relatives, neighbours, health visitors, teachers or social workers. A deliberate decision should be taken about future action. It is important for doctors to understand the procedures of other agencies, so that the full investigatory process is not triggered off prematurely. Informal discussion will be needed with a colleague or colleagues experienced in the subject, and this can often be conducted by telephone. (See paragraph 9.3).

8.3 Differential Diagnosis

It has been estimated that 15 per cent of children where non-accidental injury occurs have also been sexually abused[11].

Child sexual abuse should be remembered in the differential diagnosis of many physical conditions:—

1. Symptoms of the lower genito-urinary tract including vulvovaginitis associated with soreness and discharge; recurrent dysuria in the absence of proven urinary tract infection.

2. Genito-urinary injuries, such as vaginal bleeding, or lacerations or bruising.

3. Genito-urinary abnormalities, such as an enlarged vaginal opening or a scarred hymen.

4. Faecal soiling, retention or rectal bleeding.

5. Rectal abnormalities such as anal fissure or scars, or a lax or pouting anal sphincter.

6. Sexually transmitted disease, (see paragraph 12.21 −12.26).

7. Pregnancy in girls under sixteen years of age especially where there is no knowledge of the identity of the father.

8.4 Behavioural or emotional grounds

The occurrence of certain types of behaviour may be a strong indication that a child has been abused, whereas other indications may merely raise a slight suspicion. The presence of a number of mildly suspicious indicators will, of course, appropriately raise more concern than a single indicator of this type. Further, behavioural and emotional indicators should be considered in association with any physical symptoms or signs, and in the context of the family setting.

Serious suspicion of child sexual abuse should be aroused when the child makes a clear, unambiguous, verbal allegation of abuse. If this is a spontaneous allegation, it would be most unusual for this to be a fabrication. Exceptions to this might be where a spontaneous allegation is made following access visits to which the child is known to be antagonistic for other reasons; or if allegations are made by an adolescent caught up in a parental dispute such as divorce or custody proceedings. This could reduce suspicion to a moderate level.

Moderate suspicion should be aroused when a child:
a. Makes a verbal allegation of abuse, but in ambiguous terms, so that it is not clear precisely what sort of experience the child is describing.
b. Is sexually provocative to adults or reveals detailed knowledge of sexual matters in conversation, fantasy, or drawings, or appears preoccupied with sexual fantasies and behaviour. It should, however, be remembered that most normal children are curious about sexual matters and this will be reflected in their play. In younger children, there will, however, not be detailed knowledge of adult sexuality nor will such children be preoccupied with the topic.
c. Responds to questioning by describing sexual abuse, but has not made a spontaneous allegation. In such a situation, suspicion would become serious if spontaneous extension of the description of the occurrence was provided, together with convincing circumstantial details.
d. Shows a specific fear — eg of a father, step-father or older, sexually mature brother.

Mild suspicion should be aroused by a child who:
a. Shows a behavioural or emotional disturbance for which no other obvious cause is present.
b. Shows unexplained changes of behaviour.
c. Is fearful of men.
d. Makes a suicidal attempt for which no obvious cause is detected.
e. Runs away from home when there is no obvious cause. It should be noted that child sexual abuse may be an aetiological factor in any child disturbance.

It should be routinely included in the checklist of possible indicators along with the more usually considered stresses (eg school failure, undue parental pressure to succeed, adverse temperamental characteristics in the child, dysharmonious family relationships or brain dysfunction).

8.5 The Family Setting

A particular type of family setting should not, on its own, be regarded as grounds for serious suspicion in the absence of an allegation, or physical, emotional or behavioural indicators in the child. Moderate suspicion should be aroused if
a. The child is being brought up in circumstances in which inappropriate exposure to adult sexual behaviour is occurring, eg a child living in cramped circumstances with a mother known to be a prostitute.
b. Another child in the family is known to have been sexually abused.

Mild suspicion should be aroused in family circumstances when:—
a. There is an unusually close physical relationship between father or step-father and the child, against a background of marital disharmony.
b. A child is living in a family with distorted relationships, in which the father or step-father shows an aggressive type of personality disorder or alcoholism.
c. A child is living with a parent suffering from a psychosis or other form of mental illness in which abnormal sexual ideation is a feature.

9 INITIAL RESPONSE AND STRATEGY DISCUSSION

9.1 Once any doctor suspects that child sexual abuse may have occurred, prompt discussion in confidence with a colleague in the same or another discipline is essential to decide the next step. Telephone discussion at this stage with a professional, who is working in child abuse, is likely to be most helpful in considering the differential diagnosis and planning the next step to explore the situation, and decide what needs to be done to protect the child.

9.2 Decisions should be made as to
a. who should now see the child and where.
b. which adult (family member or relative) should be with the child for support and reassurance.

c. whether a full physical examination should be made, with the likelihood of the collection of forensic evidence, and where or by whom this should be done.

9.3 The result of the initial discussion with a colleague may lead to an agreement to continue careful supervision of the situation, because the index of suspicion is not high enough to justify extending involvement to other professionals. If there is disagreement between the two colleagues or if the index of suspicion reaches a level where the doctor is still anxious, there should be a more formal discussion (usually called a strategy discussion) with other professionals who are working in local child abuse services. A decision should then be taken as to whether or not to proceed to a case conference or to review the case after a short period of time. At all times the doctor initially concerned must remain in close contact with the child and the family situation.

10   INTERVIEWING THE CHILD

10.1 The Interview at Initial Contact

Throughout this report, the need to take a careful history is emphasised. In child sexual abuse, the clinical interview might be the most important investigation and may also be extremely distressing for the child. **At initial contact it is probably best to keep interviewing to the minimum except in the case of a child who clearly wishes to have a full discussion.** The doctor will need to use his or her judgement to decide whether to see the child with their parent or other accompanying adult or alone.

10.2 The Full Interview

Attention should be given to the nature and timing of the full interview, before arrangements are made for a full physical examination of the child[12]. (See paragraph 8.1). This full interview should normally be done by social workers and police who are working on child abuse matters locally and who are experienced in interviewing children of different ages. (See also 8.1 and 13.2). It will need to be borne in mind that this interview may have a number of different functions; to obtain clinical facts, to reassure a child, and to gain information which might be used in legal proceedings involving criminal or child protection matters. All information obtained must be carefully recorded. A video recording may prevent a child having to be re-interviewed at a later stage. Once made, it becomes part of the case notes and may not be erased and can be subpoenaed for court purposes.

10.3 Specialised Interviews

The use of very specialised techniques of interview are discussed in detail in paragraph 13.3. These have been developed to help the very young or the retarded child who might not have the necessary vocabulary to demonstrate their experiences. Such techniques should never be used in a casual manner during initial referral. **They should be employed only after careful discussion by professionals who are working on child abuse matters locally.**

11 CONFIDENTIALITY AND CONSENT

11.1 Confidentiality

The Annual Report 1987 of the General Medical Council gives unequivocal advice on this matter in cases of child abuse, including child sexual abuse[13].

'PROFESSIONAL CONFIDENCE: CASES OF CHILD ABUSE

> The Council's published guidance on professional confidence states that doctors may disclose confidential information to the police who are investigating a grave or very serious crime, provided always that they are prepared to justify their actions if called upon to do so. However, a specialist in child psychiatry recently drew to the Council's attention that its guidance does not specifically address the question of whether a doctor may properly initiate action in a case of this kind, as opposed to responding to a request. Both the British Medical Association and the medical defence societies have expressed the view that in such circumstances the interests of the child are paramount and that those interests may well override the general rule of professional confidence. On the recommendation of the Standards Committee the Council in November, 1987 expressed the view that, if a doctor has reason for believing that a child is being physically or sexually abused, not only is it permissible for the doctor to disclose information to a third party but it is a duty of the doctor to do so.'

11.2 The Joint Co-ordinating Committee of the three British medical defence organisations has also prepared helpful advice which forms an *important Annex* to this Report. (See Annex B).

11.3 Confidentiality in Case Conferences

This matter is discussed in detail in Annex B, with particular reference to the role of the doctor.

11.4 Consent

Examination without consent may be held in law to be an assault. For consent to be valid it must be:

Informed ie the person giving consent is aware of what he or she is consenting to and the possible consequences.

Freely given ie without fear, threats, fraud or coercion.

11.5 Age of Consent

A child who has reached his/her 16th birthday is regarded at law as capable of giving consent (unless there is some mental incapacity to giving informed consent) and, equally important, can also refuse consent if given by an adult on his or her behalf.

11.6 Depending on their age and understanding, younger children may also be regarded by a doctor as capable of giving consent to examination or treatment. In these circumstances it is the child's consent which is relevant. The doctor should explain fully what is going to be done, and create a reassuring atmosphere.

For younger children, who are not regarded by a doctor as capable of giving consent, formal consent must be obtained from a parent or a person in whom parental rights have been vested. This needs to be done in a non-judgemental way, explaining all procedures fully. It should be made clear that all concerned, including the carers, are working together for the best interests of the child. If co-operation cannot be obtained, the doctor should consult with other professionals concerned with the case. In the rare case where it is believed that this is an emergency situation, the doctor must decide whether to proceed without consent. The situation is no different from any other emergency in medical practice. If it is decided that this is not an emergency and consent is still being refused, then consultation with the social services department will be needed to decide whether action is required to transfer parental rights to the local authority or to a court.

11.7 Consent is equally *valid* whether given *orally* or in *writing* provided it is informed consent and freely given. Written consent is obviously preferred in many instances, as, duly witnessed, it is a permanent record to be used or referred to if necessary at a later date. It is nearly always routinely asked for when an anaesthetic is to be administered. However, oral consent is equally valid if it satisfies the foregoing conditions. Preferably it should be given in the presence of a responsible witness.

11.8 In cases where a doctor is in doubt about the duty of confidentiality or the need for consent the professional secretariat of the medical defence organisations are available for advice (see Annex B).

12 PHYSICAL EXAMINATION

Initial Examination

12.1 In many cases of suspected child sexual abuse, the child may initially be seen by a doctor who has not had specialist training in this area. A typical example might be the disclosure of problems and worries by the mother of a child to her Health Visitor. The Health Visitor may refer them to the child's family doctor or to a Community Health Doctor. The doctor's duty in such a case is to take a careful medical and social history, including any presenting symptoms. At this stage, only a general examination is required, with a visual inspection of the genital areas depending on the history, and the age and distress of the child. A careful record should be made.

12.2 If the history and circumstances indicate suspected child sexual abuse, the referring doctor will then wish to arrange an appointment with a paediatrician and/or police surgeon as soon as practicable. Discussion with professionals working in local child abuse services about strategy will also be important at this stage. (See paragraph 9.3).

Full/special examination and interpretation of physical findings

12.3 In some areas paediatricians and police surgeons are very successfully conducting physical examinations in collaboration. It is hoped that this method of working will be extended **so that the number of examinations to which a child is subjected is kept to a minimum.**

12.4 The examination should take place in a room with suitable equipment and facilities for screening for sexually-transmitted diseases and for collecting forensic specimens. The room should be quiet and away from the hurly-burly of a busy clinical area. It should also be a room in which clinical photography is possible. This examination should not take place in a police station, the one possible exception being when a child rape victim has reported to a police station, which has proper medical facilities and a victim support suite. In such instances it might be preferable to carry out the examination in that location as soon as possible in order to avoid losing trace evidence.

12.5 The doctors undertaking the examination should be trained in the examination of children and have learnt the skills needed for collecting forensic evidence. Sexual offences kits are provided by police/forensic laboratories. Hospital swabs and containers should not be used. Forensic specimens should be handed to a police officer, but legal requirements are met if the officer is outside the examination room and the specimens passed to the officer immediately after they have been obtained. Forensic laboratories do not usually screen for all sexually-transmitted diseases and additional provision may, therefore, have to be made for the collection of some of these specimens (See 12.21 – 12.26).

12.6 Doctors undertaking the examination should be willing to attend case conferences and should also be prepared to provide statements for social services and the police as well as to attend court for criminal and/or child protection proceedings.

12.7 The gender of the doctor is usually less important than the manner of the examination. However, children should be given the choice of being examined by a doctor of the same gender if this is feasible. The doctor should, if possible, get consent from the child's parent or guardian and before proceeding should give the child an explanation and gain their co-operation. This is particularly important if the child and/or parents are referred to the doctor by the social services department or other agency, especially if the child and family are not known to the doctor. When the child is over 16 only the child's consent is required (see 11.5 and 11.6 and Appendix B). The child should be allowed to have a trusted adult with them during the medical examination.

12.8 It is important that the child has an opportunity to give details of the alleged abuse prior to the medical examination, and in any case, the doctor should have a clear history of the alleged incident. Careful note should also be taken of any disturbances of micturition, bowel habit, history of threadworms, discharge, bleeding and redness. Although these conditions may be due to other causes it should be remembered that sexually abused children may well have disturbances of micturition or bowel motions and soreness as part of the symptoms of the abuse. The history will also influence whether forensic specimens should be collected. During the first 72 hours forensic specimens — eg for presence of spermatozoa in the vagina or rectum and blood for blood grouping — should always be collected, but after this interval there is little value in subjecting the child to this process.

12.9 **A general physical examination which will include throat, eyes, ears, chest and abdomen should precede the examination of genitalia and anus.** Time should be given to set the child at ease, so that examination of genitalia and anus is seen as a routine part of the procedure. Often nothing more than a thorough visual inspection of the genitalia and anus is required, possibly using the magnification of an illuminated hand lens or an auriscope without a speculum. A case can be made for the use in skilled hands of graduated glass rods to evaluate hymenal opening dimensions and to visualize hymenal tears. Such data could make a valuable contribution to the recognition of minor signs of child sexual abuse.

Digital examination of the vagina in a pre-pubertal child is rarely indicated, and where it is felt to be necessary some doctors would consider it an indication for examination under anaesthesia. Such an examination should never be lightly undertaken.

12.10 Throughout the examination the child should be talked to and given an explanation of what is happening. A spare set of swabs should be available so that the child can see and touch these if specimens are to be collected. At the end of the examination the findings should be discussed with the child, and at this stage all children should be given an opportunity to share their anxieties with the examining doctor.

12.11 Careful documentation of the results of the physical examination is required. The child's height and weight should be recorded on a centile chart. The results of the general examination should be recorded. Comments should be made on the child's demeanour and behaviour during the examination. Notes should be made of any comments made by the child.

12.12 In examining the child for injuries, particular attention must be paid to bruises, burns and bites. With child sexual abuse these are especially significant around the genitalia, thighs, lower abdomen and groin. Grip marks may also be evident around the upper arms and knees. Bruising and redness of the perineum may be found in recent assault.

12.13 It is relatively uncommon to find injuries of the penis and testes. However, tears of the foreskin frenulum will occasionally be seen. In older girls the breasts must be examined for injury and bite marks. Any physical injuries should be documented using a chart and diagrams.

Injuries to the female genitalia are also best shown on a diagram. The labia must be examined for reddening and bruising in acute abuse and for reddening and signs of chronic friction in chronic abuse. The vulva should be examined for abrasions, tears, bruises and oedema, whilst the hymen and the posterior fourchette must be examined for tears. In cases of old or recurrent abuse the tears may be replaced by scars. In the unusual case where there is vaginal bleeding the examination may be better performed under anaesthetic. Notice should be taken and a recording made of the shape, appearance and size of the hymenal opening. It is generally agreed that the normal hymenal opening before the onset of puberty is less than 0.7cms.

In some cases, clinical photography might be necessary to record important physical signs which may alter with the passage of time.

12.14 The appearance of both genitalia and anus should be carefully documented in all children with measurements of dimensions when appropriate. The significance of certain findings may only become apparent later.

Therefore, all injuries and positive physical signs should receive careful follow up, and the rate and extent of healing noted, again using diagrams. Such follow up visits will provide an opportunity to reassure the child and family that physical problems are resolving satisfactorily, and may help to clarify an equivocal diagnosis.

12.15 Other Co-existent Signs and Symptoms

Either at referral, or during the physical examination, signs and symptoms of other conditions may be complained of or found. Examples are constipation, threadworms, non-specific soreness in the genital regions, or conditions in the mouth. All should be carefully recorded, and prompt medical treatment and follow up instituted. There may be other conditions or illnesses also present, such as malnutrition, chest infection and asthma, and again arrangements for medical treatment and follow up should be made. Such arrangements should not be forgotten or overshadowed by the procedures necessary in the investigation of possible child sexual abuse.

12.16 Anus

In child sexual abuse there may be no abnormal physical signs to be detected, but in acute abuse there may be reddening and bruising around the anus. If tears occur, they are usually multiple but if they are single then they are usually posterior. There may be swelling of the margin of the anus and there may also be dilated veins, either in a complete ring around the anus or in an arc around part of the circle. With chronic abuse there may well be scars and skin tags and anal tone may be poor. The anus may be gaping with poor anal tone or may actively dilate when the buttocks are parted (so called reflex anal dilatation — see 12.18 below).

12.17 There is some controversy over the place of digital rectal examination. The difference in clinical practice should be respected, each case being judged on its individual merits, but the examining doctor should have a clear idea of what helpful physical signs may be expected. It should be remembered that a child may perceive digital insertion as an assault.

12.18 Reflex Anal Dilatation

This is *not* a new test and has been well known to forensic physicians for many years.

In older text books on forensic medicine, it was called the lateral buttock traction test[14]. It was applied mainly to adults, and when positive, indicated chronic buggery. The old name of the test was a misnomer, as it is important that no traction is used.

Methodology in children

The left lateral position is preferred by many doctors as ideal for examination of the anus. Some experts feel that the knee elbow position should be avoided as it could lead to a vivid recall of events by a child who had suffered buggery. It is for the examining doctor to decide the most appropriate position. The response of the child will largely determine the decision.

With the child usually in the left lateral position, and asked to roll up into a ball, the buttocks are gently separated. In a positive test, within a short time (up to 30 seconds) the external sphincter relaxes so that the interior of the anal canal and lower rectum can be seen. The dilatation should remain for at least 2–3 seconds, and should be distinguished from reflex puckering of the anus which occurs momentarily — the 'winking anus', — which is a natural phenomenon, especially if the rectum is full.

Some doctors now believe[15] that reflex anal dilatation occurs as a result of a stretching injury of the internal sphincter, as the external sphincter working alone can only maintain closure for about 10 seconds; ie the test is a way of demonstrating an *internal* sphincter which has been made lax due to the trauma of retrograde penetration.

The significance of reflex anal dilatation in the young child has not been fully elucidated. There is as yet no proof that it is or is not pathognomic of child sexual abuse, but when elicited it should raise the level of suspicion.

12.19 In both acute and chronic child sexual abuse there may be no physical signs. No one physical sign should be given undue importance on its own. In those cases where physical signs are present, it is advisable for the child to be seen again at a later date for reassessment.

12.20 **It cannot be emphasised too strongly that no physical sign can at the present time be regarded as being uniquely diagnostic of child sexual abuse.**

Sexually Transmitted Diseases

12.21 The diagnosis of a sexually transmitted disease in a child gives rise to a high index of suspicion of child sexual abuse. On setting up a service for children with suspected child sexual abuse, it is necessary to have discussions with local microbiology/STD laboratories. Special swabs and techniques are required to culture relevant organisms. Consideration should be given to having packs made up which will enable screening for, at least, gonorrhoea, trichomonas and chlamydia.

12.22 The presence of trichomonas and gonorrhoea is certainly highly suggestive of child sexual abuse. Gonorrhoea may be found in the pharynx, as well as in the genital and rectal areas. The relevance of chlamydia infection is at present uncertain but should raise suspicion.

12.23 Condyloma acuminata (genital warts), found in both genital and anal regions, must raise a suspicion of child sexual abuse. Diagnosis will be more specific as typing of the virus becomes more readily available.

12.24 A diagnosis of herpes genitalis should also arouse suspicion, when found in either the vulval or perianal regions.

12.25 Facilities should be available to screen for syphilis where appropriate. Presence of this organism would make sexual abuse highly probable.

12.26 The aim should be to test for the organisms discussed above in appropriate cases without subjecting the child to multiple examinations. Thus it is important that both forensic skills and laboratory facilities are available. In some Districts, the medical examination is undertaken jointly by a paediatrician and a police surgeon skilled in forensic techniques.

12.27 In cases where there is disagreement, the doctors undertaking the examination should first of all discuss and identify their differences. If these cannot be resolved, there may have to be further discussions with other professionals working on the case. The interests of the child must not be overlooked.

13   THE ROLE OF THE PSYCHIATRIST

A complete assessment requires attention to be paid not only to a child's developmental status and the quality of relationships within the family but also to the child's psychiatric state. The role of the child and adolescent psychiatrist is to diagnose and treat emotional and behavioural disorders in children, but this does not mean that all cases of CSA need to be referred to psychiatrists. Whether or not to refer should be considered under two headings:
a.   When sexual abuse is known to have occurred.
b.   When the possibility has been raised that sexual abuse has occurred.

13.1 When Sexual Abuse has definitely occurred

Child sexual abuse can be followed by a variety of severe psychiatric disorders which can, if untreated, have serious long term effects. CSA is rarely seen in isolation and is very often accompanied by physical and/or emotional abuse and neglect.
a.   Following a serious sexual assault on a child, there may be an acute post-traumatic stress disorder with emotional symptoms (anxiety and depression) or acting out (eg overdoses or running away). An urgent referral should be made in such cases.
b.   Where sexual abuse has been prolonged and in particular when it has been perpetrated by a family member, the child may well show a pattern of grossly abnormal behaviour with impairment of functioning in virtually all aspects of its life. Successful treatment of such a child will require the collaboration of professionals from many disciplines. A

psychiatric assessment should be arranged as soon as possible to determine what, if any, forms of specific psychiatric treatment might be included within the overall programme.
c. In cases where there is confirmation that sexual abuse has occurred, referral to a child psychiatrist should *not* be automatic. If the child is coping well at home and at school and has a good relationship with a parent or substitute parent, excessive intervention might well be counter-productive.
d. The child psychiatrist, skilled in family work, may have an important role in helping the entire family, including occasionally the perpetrator, to come to terms with the abuse. Where the perpetrator is a family member this may involve trying to re-establish the relationship with the abused child on a healthier basis.

13.2 When there is doubt about Child Sexual Abuse

Psychiatric techniques do not lend themselves easily to purely investigatory procedures, ie to determine whether abuse has occurred. The indications for referral should be similar to that for any other situation, namely that there is a significant psychiatric disorder which requires investigation and treatment. In these cases, however, the alerting signs of CSA (see 8.4 and 8.5) will be present and should be specifically drawn to the attention of the psychiatrist. If no psychiatric disorder is present but an investigation is requested by a parent, referral should be made not to a psychiatrist but to a professional — eg a social worker or police officer who is working in child abuse locally — if the indications for this are sufficiently strong. In some cases, a referring doctor might wish to discuss with a psychiatrist whether the child's comments or parents' allegations warrant such a referral: eg if the child has a significant developmental delay or if a child's behaviour can be seen as part of normal psycho-sexual development (see also Section 9).

13.3 There are a number of specialised interviewing techniques, sometimes called facilitation, the aims of which are to make it easier for young children to describe their experiences of CSA. The possibility that they might be harmful to children must be considered.

13.4 These techniques and the use of anatomically correct dolls and of leading questions are controversial, and there are few data on their validity. Such techniques should be used only by people who are highly experienced and trained in communicating with children and would be able to justify their use and findings in court. It is essential that only one in-depth interview with the child be carried out. If the psychiatrist intends conducting such an interview, he should inform colleagues from other disciplines, who should have the opportunity of observing it either through a one-way screen or on a video-tape.

14 ROLE OF THE FAMILY DOCTOR (See flow chart in Appendix C)

14.1 Family doctors may be involved in CSA either because they suspect the diagnosis in one of their patients or when they are contacted by a professional colleague for their comment.

14.2 When there is a suspicion that a child has been subjected to CSA the advice given in paragraph 12.1 on initial history taking applies equally to the family doctor. The family and its medical and social data are often known to the doctor who may be well known to the family. Nevertheless, it is essential for the doctor to remember the importance of written records in any subsequent legal proceedings. It is therefore vital that the initial history is recorded in detail and not merely memorised.

14.3 The initial examination by the family doctor should also follow the guidelines as advised in this report. It is important that in a suspicious case the family doctor should at an early stage consider consulting with a professional colleague of his/her choosing, to assist in deciding whether to refer for a specialist opinion. The professional colleague should be experienced in the diagnosis and management of such cases (see also Section 9).

14.4 When as a result of careful history taking and the initial physical examination the family doctor refers the child for a specialist opinion, the referral letter should be clear and non-ambiguous, for this might well become a document required in a legal process. It is often helpful for the family doctor to discuss the case with the specialist to whom the referral is being made.

14.5 When the specialist opinion has been given to the family doctor, a decision should be made by the two in consultation about whether a strategy discussion with other agencies is needed to decide if a case conference should be held.

14.6 In those cases where the family doctor is convinced that CSA has occurred the process of consultation with a colleague and referral may need to take place very quickly. The strategy discussion in which information is asked of other agencies may, in such circumstances, be by telephone.

14.7 It is unwise for family doctors to keep a suspicion of CSA to themselves and take full responsibility without consulting others, especially as they may be unaware whether other agencies have knowledge which could be relevant and important.

14.8 If the family doctor is the person who initially deals with the case, it is for them, as in other cases, to decide which specialist the child is referred to or with whom the case is discussed.

14.9 The family doctor should always remember that preconceptions must be avoided. Because a family has other problems this does not mean that CSA has occurred, nor because the family doctor knows the family well and they appear highly respectable, can CSA ever be absolutely discounted.

14.10 **The same principles of confidentiality described in section 10 and Appendix B apply equally to the family doctor.** In this respect section 10 and Appendix B are important and must be read. If the family doctor has information which is relevant to the diagnosis of CSA, whether supporting or contradicting the diagnosis, they should be prepared to share the information with professional colleagues, who may include social workers and police. This is because it is in the best interests of the child. If the doctor feels that he has certain knowledge of CSA, then he is under an obligation to the child to reveal that knowledge.

14.11 Family doctors in many instances have unique knowledge of individual family dynamics and such knowledge should be available to case conferences and other consultations. Therefore the family doctor's attendance at case conferences is clearly important. If attendance is impossible then they should at least discuss the situation, perhaps by telephone, with the chairman of the case conference. The family doctor must attend any court proceedings when required.

15 TRAINING

15.1 Undergraduate

There is, at the present time, a lack of knowledge amongst doctors about the normal anatomical appearance of female genitalia during childhood and also about the methodology of examination. There is also a lack of knowledge about the genital and anal physical signs which might be expected in cases of child abuse. It is therefore recommended that attention be given in our medical schools to the ways in which these basic facts can be taught. In addition, it is hoped that undergraduates will have an opportunity of observing the way in which cases of suspected CSA are dealt with at both a clinical and administrative level. **This teaching should be part of every undergraduate's experience.** It is for individual medical schools to decide the methods by which this teaching can be introduced, and it is hoped that in time more visual aids and video material will become available. **It will facilitate the legal aspects of the subject if there could be agreement on and conformity in the anatomical terms used to describe the details of genital and anal anatomy.**

15.2 Postgraduate

Postgraduate training should cover CSA particularly for front-line hospital staff and family doctors who may well be the first to suspect child sexual abuse. It should include multi-disciplinary seminars, so that the roles of other agencies become familiar. Time should also be set aside for discussions, within a medical setting, on the clinical picture and the significance of physical signs and their absence. Most doctors need more training in the forensic requirements of sexual abuse, both on the technical side involving the collection of specimens, and in the giving of evidence and the provision of appropriate reports. (See Appendix E).

15.3 Further Inservice Training

For those likely to be working in the field of child sexual abuse, further training is needed along five main lines:—
i. Suspecting sexual abuse and being aware of the strengths and weaknesses of the physical signs.
ii. Becoming more aware of the role of other agencies and how medical involvement contributes to the whole picture.

iii. The collection of specimens and forensic knowledge.
iv. The writing of reports and giving evidence in court. (See Appendix E).
v. It would be useful if doctors could gain experience of interviewing children of different ages and levels of ability.

15.4 Training Materials

A number of organisations and individuals are beginning to develop a range of materials, including videos. These are set out in Appendix F. Videos should always be used in conjunction with the accompanying booklet and training notes, and an experienced trainer should run the session.

16 RESEARCH

So little is known about the epidemiology of CSA that every effort must be made to collect reliable statistics especially with regard to the incidence of the condition. The figures might well vary by reason of social and geographical environment.

At all clinical levels research should be directed to the normal variations which occur in the anatomy of the genitalia during childhood. In addition more knowledge about anal and rectal physiology is required.

Even if diagnosis of CSA is made accurately, there exists the possibility of emotional damage to children and of damage to family integration and happiness by the manner in which the situation is dealt with. It is therefore important that the outcome of cases is monitored in respect of the child and family. In addition careful records must be kept of the mode of presentation and the process of diagnosis, investigation and treatment.

An important subject for psychiatric research should be the validation or otherwise of facilitation interviews and the use of anatomically correct dolls, about both of which there is some concern.

17 STAFFING IMPLICATIONS

17.1 It has been stated elsewhere in this report that CSA is an important problem which hitherto has remained very largely undiagnosed. It is hoped that, as happened with NAI, the children who previously suffered without recognition or help will in future be identified and their needs met according to the principles and guidance given in our document. It must be recognised, however, that the greater part of the medical input to the suggested multi-disciplinary approach will be provided by the community and hospital paediatricians and by child psychiatrists. The time of hospital paediatricians is already fully committed to meeting the clinical needs of children in their districts, and in most districts child psychiatrists already have difficulty in meeting the needs of child and family psychiatry. Many health districts do not as yet have any consultant community paediatricians. Furthermore training programmes are few and far between.

17.2 Each case of CSA results in far greater time involvement in court appearances for the clinician than the majority of other clinical disorders. There must be a realistic approach as to how the system we advise for dealing with child sexual abuse can be enabled to function with the efficiency which the seriousness of this condition demands. We believe that all districts should assess their needs for consultant community paediatricians.

17.3 Involvement in Court Proceedings

Some doctors find that delays or postponements in court proceedings interfere with their routine clinical work, much of which is of vital importance. It is suggested that if such problems arise, discussion should take place with the administrator of the appropriate judicial circuit or Clerk to the Justices to ensure minimal interference with other professional commitments.

17.4 These cases, especially when they progress to and beyond the case conference, produce a heavy demand on secretarial and other support services.

18 CONCLUSIONS AND RECOMMENDATIONS

These are listed as they occur in the text.

1. Widespread recognition of CSA has occurred only recently (Paragraph 2.1).

2. In child sexual abuse physical signs occur in only a proportion of cases. Medical aspects are only one element in the diagnostic process (Paragraph 2.3).

3. Cases of child sexual abuse require close co-operation and exchange of information between the services, agencies and different professions concerned with the overall well-being of children (Paragraph 2.4).

4. The diagnosis must be made and action taken against the knowledge that a mistaken diagnosis can be destructive to future child and family happiness, yet failure to recognise the problem can have serious lasting effects (Paragraph 2.5).

5. The statistics available on prevalence and incidence of child sexual abuse are unreliable (Section 3).

6. No one body, group, organisation or individual can be solely responsible for identifying cases of child sexual abuse. Therefore the administrative and management procedures which follow such identification must be integrated (Paragraph 4.1).

7. All doctors including family doctors should be familiar with the local ACPC policy and the DHA handbook. DHAs should make copies of the handbook available as necessary (Paragraph 4.3).

8. Departments involved in CSA should identify named doctors who are responsible for implementation of policy in their department (Paragraph 4.4).

9. Doctors with the necessary skills should be identified to deal with the clinical aspects of CSA (Paragraph 4.4).

10. It is no longer reasonable for any doctor to expect never to see a case of CSA, and all doctors should consciously raise their awareness of the subject (Paragraph 5.1).

11. Just as with every other condition, accurate diagnosis depends on a careful history and relevant clinical examination. The diagnosis of CSA cannot be made on physical signs alone (Paragraph 5.2).

12. Repeated clinical examinations at the initial stage should be avoided (Paragraph 5.3).

13. Medical assessment should be part of a multi-disciplinary process which includes a full family and social history (Paragraph 5.5).

14. Confidentiality is defined in the same terms for all doctors and they should be prepared to justify their actions. Medical confidentiality must not work against protection of the child who should be seen clearly as the patient (Paragraph 5.6).

15. It is the responsibility of the doctor to seek further advice and information and keep an accurate record of what is known or has been found. The doctor should contribute to case conferences and attend court if requested (Paragraph 5.8).

16. Most doctors will require updating and further training especially in the subject of normal child anatomy. Doctors who are likely to be involved in the full physical examination may need training in the collection and presentation of evidence (Paragraphs 5.9 and 4.4).

17. In cases of child sexual abuse parents should receive the same consideration as is given in all other cases in clinical practice (Section 6).

18. Immediate removal of the child to a place of safety must be weighed against the damage separation can do and is not necessary in the majority of cases (Paragraph 7.1).

19. What the child says should be taken seriously and time should be spent listening to what the child has to say (Paragraph 8.1).

20. Doctors should understand the procedures of other agencies so that the full investigatory process is not triggered off prematurely (Paragraph 8.2).

21. Child sexual abuse should be remembered in the differential diagnosis of many physical conditions (Paragraph 8.3).

22. Child sexual abuse should be considered as a possible reason for certain types of behaviour, with the level of suspicion being serious, moderate or mild depending on the type of behaviour (Paragraph 8.4).

23. A doctor who suspects that abuse has occurred should know who to consult and the next steps to be taken (Section 9).

24. The full interview of the child in a suspected case of child sexual abuse should be carried out by those experienced in the interviewing of children of different ages (Paragraph 10.2).

25. Doctors should be aware of the General Medical Council's guidance on confidentiality and the advice from the Joint Co-ordinating Committee of the UK Medical Defence Organisations (Section 11 and Appendix B).

26. The arrangements for collaboration between paediatricians and police surgeons should be extended, so that the child is subjected to a minimum of physical examinations (Paragraph 12.3).

27. The examination should take place in a specially equipped room. It should not take place in a police station, with the possible exception of a child rape victim who has reported to a police station which has proper medical facilities and a victim support suite (Paragraph 12.4).

28. The gender of the doctor is less important than the manner of examination but children should if possible be given the choice of being examined by a doctor of the same gender (Paragraph 12.7).

29. The child should have an opportunity to give details about the alleged abuse (Paragraphs 12.8 and 10.1).

30. There is little value in subjecting the child to collection of forensic specimens — eg for presence of spermatozoa — if more than 72 hours has elapsed since the incident (Paragraph 12.8).

31. A general physical examination should precede examination of the genitalia and anus (Paragraph 12.9).

32. Digital examination of the vagina in a pre-pubertal child is rarely indicated. Where it is felt to be necessary some doctors would consider it an indication for examination under anaesthesia. Such an examination should never be lightly undertaken (Paragraph 12.9).

33. The doctor should discuss the examination with the child and all children should be given an opportunity to share their anxieties with the examining doctor (Paragraph 12.10).

34. All injuries and physical signs should be carefully followed up and the extent and rate of healing noted (Paragraph 12.14).

35. Co-existent signs and symptoms must be recognised and prompt medical treatment and follow-up instituted (Paragraph 12.15).

36. Reflex anal dilatation has been well known to forensic physicians for many years. However, at the present time a positive reflex anal dilatation test is not diagnostic of CSA, but it should raise suspicion (Paragraph 12.18).

37. No one physical sign should be given undue importance on its own, and at the present time no physical sign can be regarded as being uniquely diagnostic of CSA (Paragraphs 12.19 and 12.20).

38. The diagnosis of a sexually transmitted disease in a child should give rise to a high index of suspicion of CSA (Paragraph 12.21).

39. When developing the service for children with suspected CSA it is necessary to have discussions with the local microbiology/STD laboratories (Paragraph 12.21).

40. If CSA has caused serious behavioural or emotional disturbance in the child, an urgent referral to a child psychiatrist is required. There is no need however for all cases to be referred routinely. (Paragraph 13).

41. Care should be taken in the use of specialised interviewing techniques and anatomically correct dolls. Such techniques should be used only by people who are experienced and trained in communicating with children, and who would be able to justify their findings (Paragraph 13.4).

42. It is unwise for family doctors to keep a suspicion of CSA to themselves and take full responsibility without consulting others, especially as they may be unaware whether other agencies have knowledge which could be relevant and important (Paragraphs 14.3–7, 14.10 and Appendix C).

43. Family doctors in many instances have unique knowledge of individual family dynamics, and such knowledge should be available to case conferences and other consultations. Therefore the family doctor's attendance at case conferences is clearly important (Paragraph 14.11).

44. Medical schools should include more teaching on normal anatomical appearances of the genital and anal regions in children and on child sexual abuse (Paragraph 15.1).

45. There should be agreement on and conformity in the anatomical terms used to describe the details of genital and anal anatomy (Paragraph 15.1).

46. Postgraduate training should cover child sexual abuse. It should include multi-disciplinary seminars (Paragraph 15.2).

47. Further research is necessary into the subject of child sexual abuse (Section 16).

48. All Districts need to assess their staff requirements to provide an effective service for cases of child sexual abuse (Paragraphs 17.1 and 17.2).

49. Problems over delays or postponements in court proceedings and the effect on a doctor's routine clinical work should be discussed with the circuit administrator or Clerk to the Justices (Paragraph 17.3)

Appendix A

Members of the Working Party

Professor C Eric Stroud	Professor of Child Health, Kings College Medical School, London (Chairman).
Dr H Baderman	Consultant Physician and Consultant in Accident & Emergency, University College Hospital, London.
Dr P Barbor	Consultant Paediatrician, University College Hospital, Nottingham.
Dr S Carne CBE	General Practitioner and Police Surgeon, London.
Dr H de la Haye Davies	General Practitioner and Police Surgeon, Northampton.
Professor P Graham	Professor of Child Psychiatry, Institute of Child Health, London.
Professor J Lloyd	Nuffield Professor of Child Health, Institute of Child Health, London.
Dr M Lynch	Senior Lecturer (Community Paediatrics) Guys Hospital Medical School, London.
Dr M Wilson	General Practitioner, Huntington, Yorks.
Dr S Wolkind	Consultant Child Psychiatrist, Maudsley Hospital, London.

Observers

Dr D Ferguson Lewis	Senior Medical Officer, Welsh Office.
Dr H Kilgore	Senior Medical Officer, Department of Health and Social Services, Northern Ireland.
Dr D Sinclair	Senior Medical Officer, Scottish Home and Health Department.

Secretariat

Dr B S Ely	Medical Secretary	Department of Health and Security.
Miss C Baines }	Administrative Secretaries	
Mrs C Phillips		

Appendix B

Confidentiality/Child Abuse

ADVICE FROM THE JOINT CO-ORDINATING COMMITTEE OF THE UK DEFENCE ORGANISATIONS

(APRIL 1988)

(Reproduced by kind permission of the Joint Co-ordinating Committee, The Medical Protection Society, The Medical and Dental Defence Union of Scotland, The Medical Defence Union.)

Many doctors feel that they have an especial difficulty with matters of confidentiality in cases of suspected child sexual abuse. They acknowledge a responsibility of care towards the whole family and worry that their duty to the child may conflict with this.

Doctors, however, should be clear about their responsibilities in child protection. The present law on consent to treatment is as follows:

Children: In England and Wales, the Family Law Reform Act (1969) places children of 16 or over in the same position as adults for the purposes of consenting to surgical, medical and dental treatment. This is generally interpreted as giving, by statute, the right to confidentiality which cannot be broken without the patient's consent in the same way as if they were over the age of 18.

For children under 16 the law can be summarised as follows:

1. The right to confidentiality is qualified and not absolute.

2. The doctor owes a duty of care to both the parents and to the child.

3. If there is a conflict between those duties, the right of the child should prevail.

4. It is for the individual clinician to decide to which of one or more clinicians his professional duty to the patient requires him to send information.

5. If the doctor feels it is his professional duty to send a report to another doctor it is not necessary to obtain the consent of the parents. It should of course be in the interests of the child for such a report to be sent.

The dilemma in child sexual abuse arises because the doctor may well need to consult professionals from other disciplines and agencies.

Each case must be considered on its merits.
a. In some cases, there will be no dilemma. The child and a parent together may seek help from the doctor with an allegation of abuse by a third party. In these circumstances, parental consent to the sharing of confidential information with other professionals in the District Child Abuse prevention procedures will usually be readily forthcoming, especially when it is explained that confidentiality extends to the team. In any event, it must be explained to parents that the welfare and best interests of the child come first.
b. In some cases, a parent may be suspected of child sexual abuse. It is essential that well-meaning attempts to preserve confidentiality are not allowed to prevent the welfare of the child. A young child is incapable of giving informed consent to the release of information about himself and in normal circumstances such consent would be obtained from a parent on the child's behalf. If there is a reasonable suspicion that a child may be the victim of parental abuse, every possible effort should be made to obtain a parent's consent to the disclosure of information unless it would not be in the child's best interests so to do. If parental consent is not forthcoming the child's confidence may be breached. Health care workers, including doctors, should act in the child's best interests even if it may be necessary on rare occasions to release confidential information about a parent.
c. In some cases, the suspicion of child sexual abuse may be more vague. In any District, there should be medical colleagues with a special interest and expertise in the management of child sexual abuse to whom a concerned doctor is able to turn for advice in cases of possible abuse. This is a normal type of consultation which doctors frequently engage in when confronted by difficult cases in any area of child health. Once it is decided in the light of such consultation that information should be shared with other professionals and agencies, then every effort must be made to obtain parental consent unless it would not be in the child's best interests to do so. If parental consent is not forthcoming, doctors

must be guided by the principle that the safety and welfare of the child should always come first.

d. A conflict of interests may arise when there is a doctor/patient relationship between both a parent and a child. For example, if a doctor has been consulted by a wife because of injury sustained by her as a result of physical assault by her husband, and if the doctor also comes to suspect sexual abuse of the child, is he or she entitled to disclose the information relating to the wife as well as the information relating to the child? If at all possible, the doctor would be well advised to keep the two matters entirely separate and distinct.

There are rare cases when it is necessary to disclose information both to protect the child and in the public interest, eg 'sex rings'.

In all cases where a doctor is in doubt about the duty of confidentiality, the professional secretariat of the medical defence societies are available for advice.

Confidentiality in Case Conferences

It is essential that all agencies which have staff taking part in case conferences have appropriate ethical codes.

Any confidential information which it is necessary to bring to a successful case conference should be shared on a need to know basis, secure in the knowledge that such confidentiality is respected by all members ie, a mutual confidence in confidentiality. As is stated in the DHSS Draft Guidelines, 'Child Abuse — Working Together', published as DHSS guidance under cover of a statutory circular, 'ethical and statutory codes concerned with data protection are not intended to prevent the exchange of information between different professional staff, who have a responsibility for ensuring protection of children'. The contribution of doctors to case conferences is extremely valuable. Without their input, the deliberations of such a meeting are incomplete. When attending conferences they should ensure that adequate arrangements have been made for confidentiality of the written records, and for their storage and security.

There should be local agreement between health authorities and local authorities on these matters and medical members of the Joint Protection Committees/Area Review Committees, to be called Area Child Protection Committees in future, can do much to ensure that such arrangements are satisfactory.

Appendix C

Child Sexual Abuse
The Initial Medical Contact's Role (ie Family Doctor, A/E, STD etc)

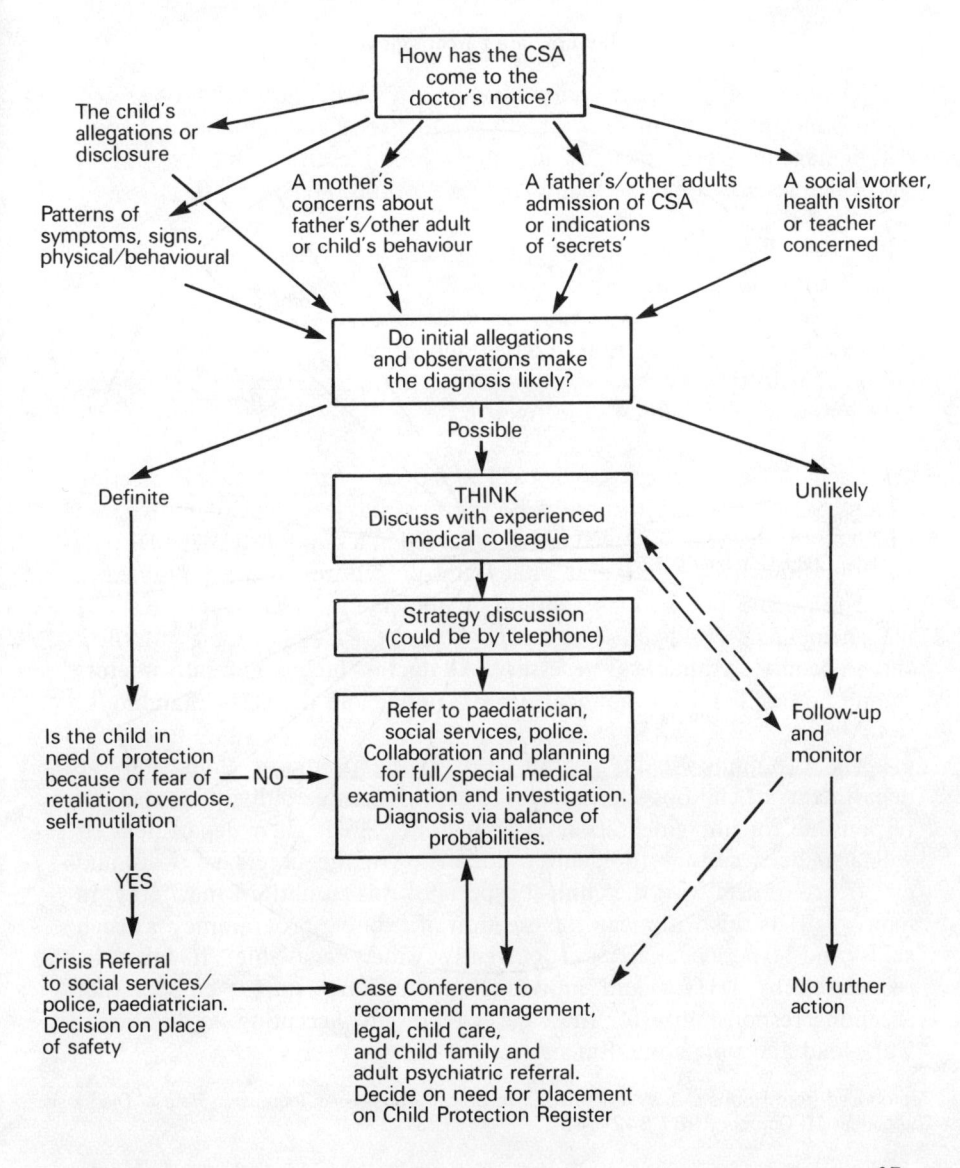

How has the CSA come to the doctor's notice?

- The child's allegations or disclosure
- Patterns of symptoms, signs, physical/behavioural
- A mother's concerns about father's/other adult or child's behaviour
- A father's/other adults admission of CSA or indications of 'secrets'
- A social worker, health visitor or teacher concerned

Do initial allegations and observations make the diagnosis likely?

- **Definite**
- **Possible** → THINK: Discuss with experienced medical colleague → Strategy discussion (could be by telephone) → Refer to paediatrician, social services, police. Collaboration and planning for full/special medical examination and investigation. Diagnosis via balance of probabilities.
- **Unlikely** → Follow-up and monitor → No further action

Is the child in need of protection because of fear of retaliation, overdose, self-mutilation —
- NO → Refer to paediatrician (as above)
- YES → Crisis Referral to social services/police, paediatrician. Decision on place of safety

Case Conference to recommend management, legal, child care, and child family and adult psychiatric referral. Decide on need for placement on Child Protection Register

Appendix D

Pie Chart Showing Relationship of Perpetrators to the Children of All Ages

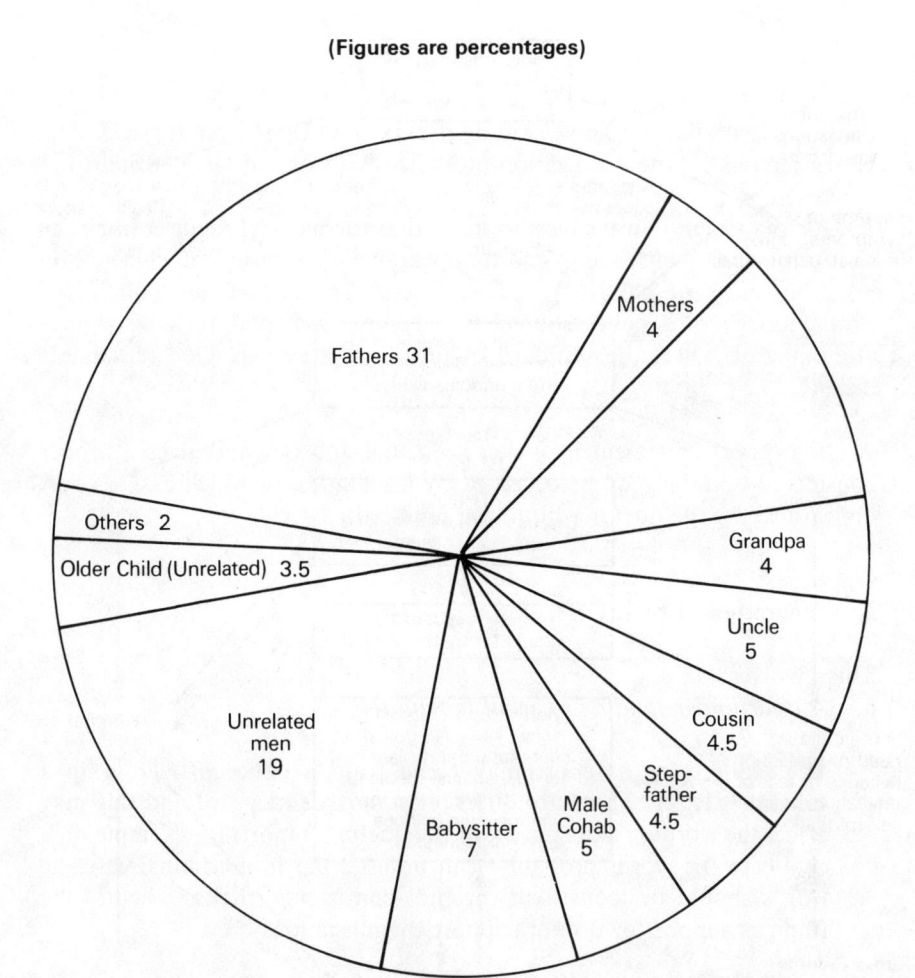

(Figures are percentages)

- Fathers 31
- Mothers 4
- Grandpa 4
- Uncle 5
- Cousin 4.5
- Stepfather 4.5
- Male Cohab 5
- Babysitter 7
- Unrelated men 19
- Older Child (Unrelated) 3.5
- Others 2

Reproduced from Hobbs C J, Wynne JM, Child Sexual Abuse – An Increasing Rate of Diagnosis. The Lancet 10 October 1987 842-845

Appendix E

The Medical Report

(This is based on lecture notes kindly provided by Dr H de la Haye Davies, Hon Secretary of the Association of Police Surgeons of Great Britain.)

1. Doctors should always bear in mind that the medical report will be the script for their subsequent court appearances: ie proof of evidence in wardship cases or child care cases, where proof is on the 'balance of probabilities'; or a police statement under the Criminal Justice Act in a criminal case where the standard of proof has to be 'beyond reasonable doubt'.

A good report or statement which is factual and fair and gives a proper considered opinion may be accepted by both sides, in which case a court appearance by the doctor will not be required.

2. **Preparation of report**

This involves:
a. *A clear understanding of what is required*

   The request for a report may come from a police officer or in a solicitor's letter. There are different standards of proof and this may affect the wording and content of the doctor's report: for example, in a civil case the word 'probably' can be used but in a criminal case the words should be 'consistent' or 'not consistent' (that is whether the findings support or do not support the allegations).

b. *Recording of the history*

   This should indicate the source of information: eg police or social worker. The history should include details of social, family and medical points as well as details about the accident/incident/allegations.

If the history is taken from the child let them tell the story in their own words. Notes should be made of all the details of physical examination and special investigations. They should be made contemporaneously, and diagrams should be drawn or photographs taken where appropriate. Where possible the doctor should consider diagnosis and, if appropriate, the prognosis.

c. *Planning the report*

The report on the findings should be as full as possible but the doctor should not exaggerate or jump to conclusions. Barristers will use the report to lead the doctor in evidence and they will then be cross examined. If the report is exaggerated or too dogmatic it might mean that the doctor 'fails to come up to proof' in the witness box. This means that the doctor finds himself having to contradict something written in the report. It is better at the rough draft stage to put in more rather than leave out what might be important later. But doctors should remember that police may edit the report to comply with the laws of evidence in a criminal case before asking for a statement under the Criminal Justice Act. The doctor will of course have to agree any such amendment and sign the final draft. In civil cases the laws of evidence are more relaxed, and the final report will probably not be altered very much from the original by the instructing solicitor.

d. *Initial draft report*

The report should start with the doctor's qualifications and experience. These should be given factually and honestly. The doctor will not be thought immodest. The court wants to know about the doctor's experience and level of expertise. A consultant will be asked more searching questions than a senior house officer and his *opinion* may then be more help to the court. On the other hand the senior house officer who, for example, first saw an injured child and properly recorded the injuries is a more reliable *witness of fact*, although the consultant (who might not have seen the child) may be able to give a more dependable opinion on those facts because of his greater knowledge and experience.

The initial draft report should mention, where applicable —

History

> Mention source, (relatives, eye witnesses, etc) but some of this might not be admissible in the final statement because of hearsay evidence rules. It is, however, better to include rather than omit and let the lawyers decide what is admissible in court.

Examination findings and diagnosis/prognosis

Finally, the report should contain the doctor's *considered opinion*, remembering that there may be alternative opinions. The doctor should therefore anticipate questions which might be asked on cross examination.

e. *Final draft*

This must be in simple language and medical jargon should be avoided. Medical terms should be translated in lay terms but it is permissible to put the medical terms in brackets afterwards, eg broken left upper arm (fractured left humerus).

It may be helpful for the doctor to discuss his/her initial draft with colleagues and/or the instructing solicitor or police where applicable so that the final draft, which is obviously an unbiased neutral record of the examination and opinions, meets the various criteria expected by the court. It is hoped that the doctor's report will be accepted by both sides so that a court appearance is unnecessary.

3. Although a police surgeon's report is the property of the Chief Constable (or the Commissioner of the Metropolitan Police) there is no legal property in a witness. Therefore the police surgeon should also, if requested, provide a report for other agencies. However, in practice it is customary in most areas for the police to provide the police surgeon's report.

Appendix F

Training Materials

1. Videos

1. *Videos* As yet, there are few quality videos which are specifically for the medical profession.

This year, the *Royal Society of Medicine* (RSM) has produced a training package, funded by DHSS, NSPCC and the Kings Fund Centre — 'Sexually Abused Children — The Sensitive Medical Examination and Management'. The package consists of a VHS video with accompanying booklet and is available from RSM Services Ltd, Film and Television Unit, 1 Wimpole Street, London, W1M 8AE. Enquiries 01 499 7422.

Leeds University has developed several training items on child abuse. Two are a VHS video and accompanying booklet on 'Medical Examinations in Child Sexual Abuse', and a further VHS Video with accompanying booklet called 'Talking with CSA Children'. Available from Audio Visual Service, University of Leeds, Leeds LS2 9JT. Enquiries 0532-431751.

2. Other Resources

i. As part of the *National Training Initiative* mounted by DHSS into aspects of training in child abuse generally, a resource known as the *Training Advisory Group on Sexual Abuse of Children* (TAGOSAC) has been centered at the National Children's Bureau. A data-base of information is being developed on training materials, courses and literature on child sexual abuse, so that information is available on request. The Development Officer can be contacted at the NCB, 8 Wakley Street, London EC1V 7QE. Tel 01 278 9441.

ii. Another part of the DHSS Initiative is providing funds to the *Open University* to produce a *basic* distance learning pack on child abuse, which includes child sexual abuse. This will be ready in 1989.

iii Many Area Child Protection Committees (formerly known as Area Review Committees) are arranging courses and seminars on the subject locally, often for multi-disciplinary and multi-agency personnel who work in this field. Addresses of those to contact should be in the local Child Abuse Handbooks.

Appendix G
References

1. 'Child Abuse — Working Together'. DHSS Guidance issued under cover of HC(88)38/LAC(88)10.

2. Schechter M D Roberge L, Sexual exploitation, In: Helfer R E, Kempe C H, eds. Child Abuse and Neglect: The Family and the Community. Cambridge Mass Ballinger 1976.

3. Kempe R S, Kempe CH, Sexual Abuse of Children and Adolescents. New York Freeman 1984.

4. Bernard Paul. Des Attentats a la Pudeur sur les Petites Filles. Paris 1886.

5. Tardieu, A. 'Etude medico-legale sur les services et mauvais traitments exercés sur des enfants' *Ann, Hyg, Pub, Med, Leg.* 1860, 13, 361–98.

6. Caffey, J. 'Multiple fractures in the long bones of infants suffering from chronic subdural haematoma' *Am, J, Roentgenol.* 1946 56(2), 163–73.

Caffey, J. 'Some traumatic lesions in growing bones other than fractures and dislocations. Clinical and radiological features'. *Brit, J, Radiology* 1957, 30, 225–38.

7. Mrazek P B, Lynch M, Bentovim A. Recognition of child sexual abuse in the United Kingdom. In Mrazek P B, Kempe CH eds. Sexually abused children and their families. London Pergamon Press, 1981 Chapter 4.

8. Mrazek D and Mrazek P B (1985) Child Maltreatment in Rutter, M and Hersov L, (Eds) Child and Adolescent Psychiatry: Modern Approaches. Blackwell. Oxford.

9. Markowe, H. The Frequency of Child Sexual Abuse in the UK. Health Trends No 1 Vol 20 Feb 1988 2–6 DHSS.

10. Finkelhor D and Associates, A Sourcebook on Child Sexual Abuse. Sage Publications 1986.

11. Vizard, E and Bentovim A. Incest — The Role of the General Practitioner. Maternal and Child Health Feb 1985 55–59.

12. Jones DPH and McQuiston M. Interviewing the Sexually Abused Child. Gaskell and Royal College of Psychiatrists. London 1988.

13. General Medical Council: Annual Report 1987 p 15.

14. Police Surgeon Journal. No 32 Dec 1987 p 46.

15. Bamford F N and Kiff E S, Letter in Lancet December 1987 p 1396.